JUMPING SPIDER

Jumping spiders care, health, diet, breeding, cages, pro's and cons and lots more included

BEN GEORGE CARRE

Table of Contents

Introduction

Greetings from the fascinating world of pet ownership—where tiny wonders may make amazing friends—the world of jumping spiders. Because of their distinct attractiveness and easy maintenance needs, jumping spiders—which are prized for their vivid colors and gregarious personality—are becoming more and more popular among pet owners.

In this investigation of "The Joyful Journey: Keeping a Jumping Spider as Your Unique Pet Companion," we set out to learn the guidelines for conscientious pet management. This guide offers helpful insights on understanding, caring for, and developing a unique bond with these interesting arachnids, regardless of experience level as a pet owner.

Learn how to build an appropriate home that closely resembles the jumping spider's native habitat to ensure that it survives in captivity. We explore the subtleties of taking care of these small but fascinating critters, from selecting the appropriate species to busting popular misconceptions.

Discover the skill of observation as you take in your jumping spider's complex habits and get a greater respect for its wit and dexterity. Our practical recommendations will improve your contact and bonding with your eight-legged friend, from feeding advice to trust-building.

Come as we explore the mysteries behind keeping jumping spiders as pets and discover the happiness, wonder, and company these amazing animals can offer.

Chapter 1

Jumping Spider Maintenance: An Orientation Guide

For aficionados of all ages, owning a jumping spider as a pet may be a fulfilling and exciting experience. These small arachnids, which are distinguished by their quickness, striking colors, and compelling mannerisms, are fascinating company. This thorough beginner's guide to jumping spider care will cover all the bases, including understanding their activities, creating an appropriate habitat, and guaranteeing their wellbeing.

1: Overview of Leaping Spiders

As members of the Salticidae family, jumping spiders are renowned for having excellent vision, which allows them to track and stalk prey with amazing precision. They are controllable and appropriate for indoor environments because to their small size, which ranges from a few millimeters to a centimeter. Jumping spiders are an interesting and engaging addition to the realm of exotic pets because of their curious and gregarious nature.

2: Selecting the Appropriate Species

It is crucial to select the appropriate species of jumping spider before delving into the world of care. Although there are many of kinds of jumping spiders, some are more frequently kept as pets because of their small size and attractive look. Marpissa muscosa, Phidippus regius (Regal Jumping Spider), and the strikingly colorful Peacock Spider (Maratus spp.) are popular options. A successful and fulfilling pet ownership journey depends on researching and choosing the species that suits your tastes and degree of experience.

3: Configuring the Environment

An essential part of caring for jumping spiders is creating an appropriate habitat. A well-thought-out enclosure permits contact and observation in addition to guaranteeing the physical well-being of the spider. Think about the following essential components:

3.1 Coverage

To stop escapes, pick a little, well-ventilated container with tight-fitting lids. The best container to watch your spider's behavior in is one that is clear. To keep the right amount of airflow, make sure there are tiny ventilation holes.

3.2 Basis

Provide your jumping spider a substrate to investigate and scurry about on at the bottom of the container. It is best to use a combination of sphagnum moss and potting soil to retain humidity without becoming unduly wet.

3.3 Accents and Hideouts

To make an environment appear more natural, add details like artificial plants, silk leaves, or tiny twigs. In order to give your jumping spider a sense of security, provide hiding places with small pieces of cork bark or empty coconut shells.

3.4 Humidity and Temperature

Keep the temperature between 70 and 75°F (21 and 24°C) and the humidity between 50 and 70%. To attain the necessary humidity, you can use a small water dish or sprinkle your surroundings frequently.

Feeding Your Jumping Spider in Section Four

By nature, jumping spiders are predators who hunt small insects for food. For their health and wellbeing, it is imperative to provide a varied and appropriate food.

4.1 Living Prey

Provide a range of live prey, including small wingless fruit flies, pinhead crickets, and fruit flies. Make sure the meal is the right size—no more than the spider's body.

4.2 Feeding Timetable

Feed your jumping spider once or twice a week, varying the amount of food depending on its size and hunger. See how it feeds to determine how hungry it is.

4.3 Dietary Add-ons

To make sure your jumping spider gets the nutrients it needs, think about dusting objects that serve as prey with multivitamin pills and calcium.

5: Monitoring Conduct and Establishing Credibility

Jumping spiders are renowned for their unusual actions and curious disposition. Establishing a connection and developing trust require taking the time to see and comprehend these behaviors.

5.1 Inquisitive Discoverers

Jumping spiders are explorers by nature. Keep an eye on how they move and engage with their surroundings. Introducing new stimuli, such as gently vibrating objects or moving prey, can pique their curiosity.

5.2 Taking Care When Handling

Although it is manageable, it is important to proceed cautiously. Because jumping spiders can be delicate, handling them too much could stress them out. If you must handle, do so carefully and near the ground to avoid falling and hurting yourself.

5.3 Dance as a Medium for Communication

Numerous jumping spiders use elaborate mating rituals. Even though these intriguing rituals are not observed in pet environments, knowing about them helps you better appreciate their intricate social structures.

6: Frequently Held Myths and Misconceptions

Like any other exotic pet, jumping spiders are not without myths. It is crucial to bust these illusions in order to practice responsible ownership.

6.1 Outrightness

Despite popular assumption, jumping spiders do not pose a threat to people. On the other hand, if they sense danger, they might act defensively. Recognizing their nonverbal cues helps reduce tension.

6.2 Performers of Escape

Even though jumping spiders are quick and graceful, having an enclosure built up correctly greatly lowers the chance of an escape. Crucial precautions include tight lids and routine inspections of the integrity of the enclosure.

6.3 Durability

Jumping spiders typically live from several months and a few years, which is a short lifespan when compared to larger spiders. This natural lifetime highlights how important it is to spend as much time as possible with these amazing animals.

7: Veterinary Care and Health Monitoring

It's essential to regularly check on the health of your jumping spider in order to identify any possible problems early on. It may be difficult to locate an exotic veterinarian with specific training, but it's crucial to recognize the warning signals of distress.

7.1 Indices of Well-Being

A jumping spider that is in good health is alert, energetic, and follows a set eating pattern. Bright colors and regular grooming are further signs of success.

7.2 Indications of Anxiety

Any noticeable anomalies, unusual lethargy, or changes in appetite should be treated right away. It is advised in such situations to seek advice from a qualified exotic pet doctor.

8: Summary

A unique and rewarding experience, owning a jumping spider as a pet provides insight into the complex world of arachnids. For those who are new to owning jumping spiders, this beginner's guide is an all-inclusive resource that covers everything from creating the ideal home to studying their behaviors and busting myths. A fulfilling relationship with your eight-legged pal will come from exercising patience, observation, and sincere interest as you negotiate the pleasures and difficulties of taking care of these little friends.

Chapter 2

Members of the Salticidae family, which include jumping spiders, are becoming more and more popular as unusual and fascinating pets. The world of exotic pet ownership is enhanced by their captivating behaviors, vivid hues, and little size. This in-depth examination of jumping spiders' special qualities, interactive nature, and delight they provide to aficionados will provide light on why they make such fascinating pets.

1: The Wonder of Tiny Marvels
The small size of jumping spiders is well known; they usually measure between a few millimeters and a centimeter. Their small size adds to their appeal and qualifies them for indoor environments. Jumping spiders are renowned for their exceptional vision and incredible

agility despite their small size. They can track and hunt prey with precision because of their remarkable visual acuity, which is facilitated by their eight eyes, which are organized in a configuration akin to that of a pair of gigantic glasses.

1.1 Brilliant Colors

The vivid and varied hue of jumping spiders is one of its most remarkable characteristics. Every species has its own color scheme, which ranges from vivid reds and yellows to metallic greens and blues. This rainbow of hues gives jumping spiders an eye-catching visual appeal that sets them apart from other arachnids.

1.2 Distinctive Anatomy

A jumping spider's little body is covered in many features and patterns, such as hairs and bristles that improve their sense of smell. Specialized features like as the hydraulically stretched legs enable them to move with purpose and agility, even making precise and controlled jumps.

2: Knowledge and Inquisitiveness

In the realm of arachnids, jumping spiders stand out due to their intellect and curiosity, which extend beyond their outward characteristics. Their attractiveness as pets is greatly enhanced by these characteristics.

2.1 Ability to Solve Problems

Studies have indicated that jumping spiders are capable of solving problems. They have been seen negotiating challenging mazes and riddles in lab settings in order to get to their prey. As they explore and adjust to varied stimuli in their captivity, their intelligence is made evident.

2.2 Interactional Patterns

Jumping spiders are distinguished from many other spider species by their social habits. They display their curiosity by reacting to outside cues like movement or vibrations. A special kind of bond is formed between the pet owner and the spider, with some devotees even reporting a degree of recognition and responsiveness to their presence.

2.3 Customs of Courtship

Jumping spiders are well known for their complex displays and dances that are part of their courting rituals. Although natural mating situations are the primary settings in which these behaviors are seen, aficionados can discover intriguing snippets of their social dynamics in a confined setting.

3: Minimal Upkeep and Space Needs

A appealing option for individuals looking for an exotic pet that fits into a hectic lifestyle or limited space is the jumping spider. They are affordable for a diverse variety of pet owners because to their small size and simple maintenance needs.

3.1 Compact Enclosure Size

Because of their small size, jumping spiders don't need large habitats. It only takes a tiny, well-ventilated container with the right substrate, embellishments, and hiding places to create the perfect setting.

3.2 Minimal Upkeep

As pets, jumping spiders require less upkeep than larger species. They are a desirable option for those with hectic schedules because of how simple it is to maintain their feeding routine, groom, and enclosure.

4: Delightful Notes & Companionship

For pet owners, watching jumping spider behavior may be a great source of delight and intrigue. Their graceful movements, cunning hunting techniques, and even silent periods make for an exciting and fulfilling encounter.

4.1 Techniques for Hunting

The ability of leaping spiders to hunt is a sight to behold. Their deliberate strides, accurate leaps, and lightning-fast reflexes when hunting present an amazing demonstration of nature at work. Seeing these actions encourages a greater understanding of the complexity of the natural world.

4.2 Developing a Relationship with Your Leaping Spider

Although many owners of jumping spiders describe feeling a sense of connection with their pets, bonding with a spider may seem like an unusual idea. Pet owners can create a connection with their animals that goes beyond conventional ideas of friendship by paying close attention to them, interacting with them gently, and getting to know their unique characteristics.

4.3 Worth of Education

For aficionados of all ages, owning a jumping spider as a pet can be an instructive experience. It offers a chance to learn about the behavior and biology of arachnids as well as the fragile environmental balance. Both adults and children can benefit greatly from this experiential learning opportunity.

5: Busting Myths and Fallacies

Like any unusual pet, jumping spiders are the subject of many myths and false beliefs. In order to ensure proper pet care and make educated decisions, it is imperative that these myths be addressed for potential owners.

5.1 Aggression

Despite what is commonly believed, jumping spiders do not pose a threat to people. They are more inquisitive than combative due to their small size and gregarious disposition, yet they may display defense actions if they feel threatened.

5.2 Art of Evasion

Although jumping spiders are agile, the possibility of an escape is greatly decreased with a well-designed enclosure. Preventive methods that work well include making sure lids are securely fastened and routinely inspecting the enclosure for integrity.

5.3 Short Life Expectancy

Compared to larger pets, jumping spiders have a shorter lifespan, usually lasting a few months to a few years. Even though they only spend a short time with their owners, the wonder and joy they provide make the encounter valuable.

6: Ethical Ownership and Relevant Factors

Just like with any animal, good pet ownership is crucial. Potential owners of jumping spiders ought to take into account a number of considerations in order to protect their eight-legged friends.

6.1 Selection of Species

It's important to select the correct species according to size, temperament, and level of experience. To give the chosen species the best care possible, it is crucial to investigate their unique requirements.

6.2 Configuring the Enclosure

It takes careful planning to create an appropriate habitat, including the right substrate, furnishings, and lighting. A healthy captivity environment is facilitated by routine observation and correction.

6.3 Animal Health

Finding an unusual veterinarian with specialized training may be difficult, but being aware of your pet's symptoms and getting help when you need it is a responsible part of pet ownership.

7: Synopsis

In conclusion, choosing to keep a jumping spider as a pet can lead to an amazing world full of unique interactions, intelligence, and miracles. Jumping spiders provide something new to the idea of unusual pets, from their vivid colors and complex activities to the delight of observation and the possibility of bonding. A sincere respect for the natural beauties these arachnids provide combined with responsible ownership turns the encounter into a voyage of delight, connection, and discovery. The appeal of jumping spiders as intriguing pets is sure to make an impression, regardless of your experience with unusual pets or if you're fresh to the world of arachnid companionship.

Chapter 3

A vital component of guaranteeing your jumping spider's general pleasure and well-being in captivity is creating the ideal habitat for it. In addition to offering your spider a secure and comfortable home, a well-designed enclosure lets you see and enjoy your spider's natural habits. We will go over every aspect of creating the perfect environment for your jumping spider in this in-depth guide, including substrate, décor, temperature, humidity, and enclosure selection.

1: Selecting the Appropriate Enclosure
Choosing a suitable enclosure is the first step toward building a home that meets your jumping spider's unique requirements.

1.1 Dimensions and Size

Select a tiny enclosure based on how big your jumping spider is. Despite their small size, it is crucial to give these spiders plenty of room to go around and explore. For the majority of jumping spider species, a container measuring roughly 6 by 6 by 6 inches is appropriate.

1.2 Airflow

To keep airflow, make sure the enclosure is well ventilated. The container's lid and sides include tiny holes that let in enough airflow without allowing too much humidity to build up.

1.3 Openness

Choose a transparent container so that you can observe your jumping spider with ease. Its activities are clearly visible through transparent walls, so you can observe its behaviors without upsetting it.

2: Selection of Substrates

Selecting the appropriate substrate is essential to establishing a cozy and authentic habitat for your jumping spider.

2.1 Sphagnum moss mixed with potting soil

Mix sphagnum moss and potting soil to create a substrate base. This mixture gives your jumping spider the right texture so it may move around and, if it so chooses, burrow.

2.2 Management of Moisture

Keep the substrate's moisture content in check. Although they don't need a lot of humidity, jumping spiders can be kept hydrated and their native habitat can be replicated with a somewhat wet substrate.

2.3 Intensity

Make sure the substrate is deep enough for your jumping spider to dig, or to make silk retreats if it so desires. Aim for a depth of about one to two inches to create a cozy and interesting setting.

3: Accents and Hideouts

Incorporate characteristics of the natural habitat of a jumping spider to improve the enclosure's aesthetic appeal.

3.1 Branches and Twigs

Incorporate tiny branches and twigs into the cage to provide climbing surfaces. Being skilled climbers, jumping spiders will welcome the opportunity to investigate vertical areas.

3.2 Man-Made Plants

Introduce artificial plants made of silk or plastic to mimic the flora that grows in their natural habitat. These additions have aesthetic appeal, but they also function as anchor points and hiding places for web construction.

3.3 Secret Locations

Add hiding places for your jumping spiders, such as little bits of cork bark or split coconut shells. This gives the spider a sense of security and permits it to withdraw when it needs alone.

4: Controlling Temperature and Humidity

Keeping your jumping spider at the right temperature and humidity is crucial to its health.

4.1 Range of Temperature

Maintain an enclosure temperature of between 70 and 75°F (21 and 24°C). The majority of standard room temperatures are fine; just stay away from sudden changes in temperature.

4.2 Percentage of Humidity

Although they don't need a lot of humidity, spraying the enclosure once or twice a week will help make the microenvironment more humid for the jumping spiders. Keep an eye on the substrate to make sure it stays just barely moist but not soggy.

4.3 Illumination

Although jumping spiders are not very light-sensitive, maintaining a natural day-night cycle can be beneficial to their health. Keep the enclosure out of direct sunlight as too much heat might be harmful.

5: Stations for Watering and Feeding

To guarantee that your jumping spider has easy access to necessary resources, create sections specifically dedicated for feeding and watering.

5.1 Refueling Area

Put little plates or containers within the enclosure to hold live prey. After feeding, these are simple to remove, keeping uneaten prey from contaminating the habitat.

5.2 Station of Watering

Fill a little dish with clean water. Because jumping spiders are little and may be dangerous in deeper water sources, use a shallow dish to avoid drowning.

6: Upholding Hygiene

To keep your jumping spider healthy and the habitat clean, regular care is essential.

6.1 Cleaning Spots

Eliminate any uneaten prey items as soon as possible to keep things clean and stop bacteria from growing. Regularly check the enclosure for evidence of pests or mold.

6.2 Substitute Substitution

Replace some of the substrate on a regular basis to maintain the environment's freshness and stop waste from accumulating. This lets you keep an eye on the enclosure's general condition as well.

6.3 Sanitization

Make sure the enclosure is completely clean before changing the substrate. To keep your jumping spider's living area clean, lightly cleanse surfaces with a vinegar and water solution.

7: Enhancement of Behavior

Enrichment activities will help your jumping spider become more mentally and physically stimulated.

7.1 New Initiations

To stimulate the curiosity of your jumping spider, introduce sporadic new stimuli, like moving objects that serve as prey or lightly tapping on the enclosure. This gives you mental stimulation as well as the opportunity to watch its deft and nimble motions.

7.2 Possibilities for Webbing

Web-building behaviors are displayed by certain jumping spiders. Provide silk-producing insects or fine silk threads to promote the development of webs, adding another level of behavioral enrichment.

8: Perception and Communication

Establishing a bond with your jumping spider requires thoughtful observation as well as polite communication.

8.1 Resilience

Without adding to the stress, study the habits of your leaping spider for a while. When letting your spider become used to its surroundings and your presence, patience is essential.

8.2 Cautious Handling

Although they may be dealt with, leaping spiders must be handled very carefully. Handling should only be done when absolutely essential, such as while maintaining enclosures. To avoid falls, interactions should always be brief and kept near to the ground.

8.3 Establishing Credibility

It takes time to establish trust with your jumping spider. Positive relationships between you and your pet are facilitated by secure, enriching environments and consistent, compassionate interactions.

Section 9: Final Thoughts

It takes careful consideration to combine behavioral enrichment, responsible care, and environmental elements to create the ideal habitat for your jumping spider. You may create an environment in which these tiny wonders can flourish and exhibit their fascinating behaviors by taking into account their particular demands and emulating their natural home. In addition to being beneficial for your jumping spider's health, creating and maintaining an excellent habitat gives you firsthand access to the fascinating world of arachnids. Making the ideal habitat for your eight-legged friend becomes a symbol of your dedication to giving them the best possible life as you set out on this path of ethical pet management.

Chapter 4

Recognizing the Behavior of Jumping Spiders:

Advice for Pet Owners

Gaining insight into jumping spider behavior is an exciting adventure that helps pet owners develop a closer bond with these amazing arachnids. The Salticidae family of spiders includes jumping spiders, which are renowned for their unusual habits, agility, and curious disposition. We will explore the nuances of jumping spider behavior in this in-depth guide, offering insightful information and helpful hints to pet owners on how to watch over, analyze, and improve the health of their eight-legged friends.

1: Agile Movements and an Inquisitive Nature

Many people are aware of jumping spiders because of their curious and gregarious nature. Pet owners can appreciate the agility and curiosity that set these spiders apart by observing these traits.

1.1 Learning through Observation

A great degree of intelligence and the ability to learn by observation are displayed by jumping spiders. Their ability to notice and absorb information from their surroundings enables them to quickly acclimate to unfamiliar situations.

1.2 Inquiry and Discovery

By giving your jumping spiders a home with lots of different things to investigate, pet owners may stimulate their natural curiosity. To pique their curiosity, introduce new stimuli like softly tapping the enclosure or providing moving prey items.

1.3 Flexible Motions

Spiders that jump are incredibly agile creatures. Their versatility is demonstrated by their ability to jump precisely and maneuver across challenging terrain. Giving them climbing possibilities, such little branches or twigs, enables them to demonstrate their deft movements.

2: Habits of Eating

It is essential to comprehend jumping spider eating habits in order to guarantee that their food is well-rounded and nutrient-rich.

2.1 Techniques for Hunting

Skilled predators, jumping spiders use unusual tactics to bring down their prey. Their keen vision allows them to track and hunt tiny insects before precisely jumping to capture them. These hunting habits can be observed to gain understanding about their innate tendencies.

2.2 The Pouncing Method

Jumping spiders are known for their pouncing skill. During their leaps, they utilize silk draglines as a safety precaution that allows them to return to a safe place if necessary. This is a behavior that pet owners can observe and enjoy during feeding times.

2.3 Identifying Signs of Hunger

It's important for pet owners to understand when their jumping spiders are hungry. When a spider is ready to eat, it will exhibit increased activity, heightened reactivity to stimuli that resemble prey, and a more attentive posture.

3 : Social Dynamics

Even though they are not very gregarious animals, jumping spiders display intriguing social behaviors, particularly when they are engaged in mating rituals.

3.1 Displays of Mating

To entice females, male jumping spiders put on lavish courtship displays. These exhibits frequently feature dexterous motions and vivid hues. One can gain insight into the social dynamics of jumping spiders by seeing these rituals.

3.2 Aggression Toward Women

Certain kinds of jumping spiders have aggressive females that target males, particularly if the males reject their advances for a mate. When necessary, pet owners can offer appropriate separation by being aware of these dynamics.

3.3 The Alone Nature

Because jumping spiders are mainly solitary animals, pet owners should be aware of their desire for private areas. Although certain species might be able to live together under certain circumstances, it's usually best to house them apart to avoid stress.

4: Body Language as a Communication Tool

Pet owners can have a better understanding of their jumping spiders' moods and habits by learning to decipher their subtle body language cues.

4.1 Protective Positions

In response to perceived threats, jumping spiders may assume protective stances. They may do these by rising their bodies, lifting their front legs, or even showing off their teeth. Pet owners can reduce their stress levels and prevent unneeded disruptions by being aware of these indicators.

4.2 Acknowledgment of Owners

Some owners of jumping spiders report recognizing their pets, however the scientific community disagrees about the amount of spider cognition. The spider and its owner may become more accustomed to each other and develop a degree of trust through regular careful handling and positive interactions.

4.3 Reaction to Outside Inputs

When faced with movement or other external cues, such as vibrations, jumping spiders react quickly. Pet owners can interact with their spiders by softly tapping the enclosure or giving them light vibrations to see how they move quickly.

5: Creating Connections and Trust

Although it may seem unusual, it is totally feasible to develop a bond with a jumping spider through polite and patient interactions.

5.1 Cautious Handling

If you must handle your jumping spider, proceed very cautiously. To minimize strain or falls, keep conversations short, keep close to the ground, and refrain from abrupt movements.

5.2 Relentless Attendance

A steady, non-intrusive presence is essential for fostering trust. Without interfering with its surroundings, observe your jumping spider for a while. This gives the spider time to gradually get used to your presence.

5.3 Encouragement in a Positive Way

Feeding is one way to provide positive reinforcement. Regular feeding and the use of live prey items can foster good associations and improve the relationship between the owner and their jumping spider.

6: Indications of Good Health

It's critical to keep an eye on your jumping spider's general health in order to identify any possible problems early.

6.1 Consistent Eating

A jumping spider that is in good health follows a set eating pattern. Unusual eating habits or an abrupt decrease of appetite could be signs of serious health issues.

6.2 Reactive Conduct

In general, a jumping spider that is sensitive and energetic indicates healthy health. An astute owner can see behavioral shifts that could indicate concern very quickly.

6.3 Brilliant Colors

A healthy jumping spider has colors that are vibrant and well-maintained. Pigmentation changes or dull colors may indicate molting, illness, or stress.

7: Enhancement of the Environment

Enriching the habitat around jumping spiders benefits their mental and physical health.

7.1 New Initiations

To stimulate the curiosity of your jumping spider, introduce sporadic new stimuli, like moving objects that serve as prey or lightly tapping on the enclosure. This gives you mental stimulation as well as the opportunity to watch its deft and nimble motions.

7.2 Possibilities for Webbing

Web-building behaviors are displayed by certain jumping spiders. Provide silk-producing insects or fine silk threads to promote the development of webs, adding another level of behavioral enrichment.

8: Possible Difficulties and Solutions

When it comes to jumping spider care, pet owners need to be aware of potential difficulties and know how to resolve frequent problems.

8.1 Acts of Aggression

Although most species of jumping spiders are not aggressive toward humans, some may act defensively. Pet owners who are aware of these tendencies can reduce stress and prevent pointless confrontations.

8.2 Concerns About Molting

Jumping spiders go through a natural process called molting. During this time, pet owners should provide a peaceful and uncluttered environment. A spider might be getting ready for a molt if it seems listless or won't eat.

8.3 Preventing Evasion

Because they are nimble, jumping spiders may try to flee. To prevent unintentional escapes, make sure enclosure lids are securely fastened, verify enclosure condition on a regular basis, and handle with caution.

9: Final Thoughts

For pet owners, comprehending the behavior of jumping spiders is a rewarding and continuous task. It entails careful observation, deference to the innate tendencies of the spiders, and a dedication to fostering an atmosphere that fosters their welfare. Through an exploration of the subtleties of their curious disposition, eating habits, social interactions, and modes of communication, owners of pets can establish a more meaningful bond with their jumping spiders. This detailed guide provides insightful advice and helpful hints to enhance the experience of taking care of these amazing arachnids. Jumping spiders are extraordinary companions in the world of exotic pets because of their curiosity, agility, and unique characteristics, which you will discover as you go on this adventure of observation, interaction, and bonding with your own jumping spider.

Chapter 5

Everything You Should Know About Feeding Your Jumping Spider

One of the most important parts of taking care of your jumping spider is feeding it, which has a big impact on its general health, vigor, and happiness. Members of the Salticidae family, jumping spiders are apex predators distinguished by their exceptional hunting abilities and distinctive feeding habits. We will go over all you need to know about feeding your jumping spider in this comprehensive guide, including appropriate prey items, feeding schedules, nutritional concerns, and typical troubleshooting techniques.

1: An Overview of the Jumping Spider Diet

As carnivorous predators, jumping spiders consume small insects as their food source. Fruit flies, tiny crickets, wingless fruit flies, and other small invertebrates make up the majority of their food. Jumping spiders aggressively pursue and capture prey in their native environments by using their acute vision and dexterity.

1.1 Innate Hunting Mechanisms

Recreating an appropriate feeding environment in captive requires an understanding of jumping spiders' innate hunting tendencies. These spiders are skilled at precisely stalking, jumping, and capturing their victim.

1.2 The Value of Living Prey

For jumping spiders to meet their nutritional needs, they must consume live prey. The spider's hunting instincts are heightened by the movement of live prey, which enriches the creature mentally and physically.

1.3 Properly Dimensioned Prey

It is important to choose prey that is the right size. To ensure that there is no risk of harm during capture and consumption, the prey item should not exceed the size of the spider's body.

2: Creating a Schedule for Feeding

Maintaining the health and vitality of your jumping spider requires that you set up a regular feeding regimen.

2.1 How Often You Feed

Due to their rapid metabolisms, jumping spiders require frequent feedings in order to maintain their energy levels. Although feeding should be done every two to three days in general, each spider's demands will differ according on its size, age, and activity level.

2.2 Tracking Your Hunger

Keep an eye on your jumping spider's hunger and modify the frequency of feedings as necessary. A healthy appetite is indicated by an active, responsive spider that eats its prey rapidly; on the other hand, a lack of interest may indicate other factors, such as stress or molting.

2.3 Abstinence Prior to Molting

Often, jumping spiders move quickly before molting. During this time, they might show less of an appetite. It's imperative to honor their normal molting process and refrain from providing food when they are fasting.

3: Items That Make Good Prey

Choosing appropriate prey items is crucial to feeding your jumping spider a healthy, well-balanced diet.

3.1 Fruit Flies

For leaping spiders, fruit flies without wings, such Drosophila hydei or Drosophila melanogaster, make ideal staple prey. They are widely available in the pet trade, tiny, and manageable.

3.2 Tiny Crickets

Another good food source for jumping spiders is pinhead or tiny crickets. To reduce the possibility of the spider becoming hurt, make sure the crickets are the right size.

3.3 Additional Small Invertebrates

Think about adding more tiny invertebrates, such springtails or tiny roaches, to the diet to vary it up. A dietary profile that is well-rounded may benefit from this variation.

4: Nutrition-Related Issues

For your jumping spider's general health and lifespan, make sure it eats a diet rich in nutrients.

4.1 Prey with a Gutload

Giving the prey items a healthy diet before presenting them to the jumping spider is known as gut-loading. This improves the prey's nutritional value, which benefits the spider's diet.

4.2 Supplements for Nutrition

Think about dusting calcium and multivitamin supplements on prey items. This is particularly crucial to prevent any inadequacies and to provide the best possible health for jumping spiders kept in captivity.

4.3 Staying Hydrated

Even while their food provides jumping spiders with the majority of their moisture, it's still a good idea to have a tiny water dish inside the enclosure. Because the spider is little, make sure the water dish is shallow to avoid drowning.

5: Methods of Feeding

It takes careful methods to feed your jumping spider in order to promote natural behaviors and guarantee a satisfying feeding experience.

5.1 Feeding by Hand

When feeding a jumping spider by hand, prey is presented to it directly using forceps or soft-tipped tweezers. This approach makes it possible to observe and engage closely with the spider, strengthening the link between it and its owner.

5.2 Search-and-Release

When prey is allowed to travel about the enclosure, the jumping spider can display its typical hunting habits. This technique stimulates the mind and body.

5.3 Swinging Prey

A soft movement of the prey in front of the spider can awaken its hunting instincts. This encourages the spider to stalk and seize its meal by imitating the actions of prey in the wild.

6: Seeing How They Feed

It's interesting to watch how your jumping spider feeds, because it can reveal important information about its health and wellbeing.

6.1 Pouncing and Stalking

Plucking and stalking are two of jumping spiders' well-known habits. Observe as they follow their prey with patience before leaping with rapid accuracy to seize it.

6.2 Using Silk in Food

When they feed, some jumping spiders make use of silk. They might build a silk refuge to consume prey or a dragline to keep themselves secure while pouncing. Their feeding routines become even more intricate as a result of this natural tendency.

6.3 Changing Out and Eating

Before molting, jumping spiders may turn down food or show signs of decreased appetite. It might be distressing to try to feed a spider when it is exhibiting this natural behavior. Give them a calm environment and respect their molting process.

7: Troubleshooting Problems with Feeding

Providing food for jumping spiders can present a number of difficulties for pet owners. The health of the spider depends on taking immediate action on these problems.

7.1 Not Wanting to Eat

If your jumping spider repeatedly declines food, there may be a number of reasons why, including stress in the habitat, disease, or molting. Assess the spider's general health and modify its surroundings as necessary.

7.2 Aggression Towards Prey

There are situations when prey objects act aggressively toward the spider. When choosing your victim, exercise caution and keep an eye on the exchange. If hostility is seen, think about presenting various prey items.

7.3 Overindulging in food

Frequent feeding is necessary, but excessive feeding can result in obesity and other health problems. In order to maintain a balance between moderation and nutrition, modify the feeding schedule in accordance with the spider's appetite and activity level.

8: Summary

One exciting and fulfilling part of taking care of your jumping spider is feeding it, which lets you see its natural activities and directly support its well-being. Your jumping spider can live in a healthy habitat if you recognize their hunting instincts, set up a regular feeding schedule, and give them a varied and wholesome diet. The relationship between a pet owner and a spider is enhanced by the attachment created via feeding interactions. You'll learn a lot about the fascinating world of jumping spiders as you set out on this voyage of mindful feeding and careful attention, building a bond with your eight-legged friend that extends beyond the feeding schedule and benefits their general health."

Chapter 6

Building Trust and Connection with Your Jumping Spider to Form a Bond

Establishing trust and connection with your jumping spider requires understanding their behavior, providing a suitable environment, and engaging in positive interactions. Jumping spiders are small arachnids that are known for their agility and curious nature. Nevertheless, these arachnids can make delightful companions when approached with care and patience.

Comprehending the Behavior of Jumping Spiders:

Scientifically classified as members of the family Salticidae, jumping spiders are distinguished by their distinct appearance and unique hunting strategy. These spiders have large, forward-facing eyes and an amazing ability to jump, which shows a level of intelligence not often associated with arachnids. It is important to understand their behavior in order to create a positive and comfortable environment for them.

While many other spider species build webs to catch prey, jumping spiders actively hunt, using their keen eyesight and agility to pounce on their prey. This natural behavior serves as the foundation for developing a bond based on mutual understanding and respect. Jumping spiders are naturally curious and frequently exhibit inquisitive behaviors such as exploring their surroundings and reacting to external stimuli.

Creating an Appropriate Environment:

Establishing the best possible environment for your jumping spider is crucial to its health and can greatly aid in the development of trust. To start, choose an enclosure that provides enough ventilation and room for the spider to roam around. A compact terrarium with a tight-fitting lid and tiny holes for good ventilation is a great option.

Place a variety of surfaces for climbing and hiding, such as small twigs, leaves, or pieces of bark; these elements provide the spider with enrichment and opportunities to display its natural behaviors. Add substrate, such as coconut fiber or peat moss, to the bottom of the enclosure to mimic their natural environment.

Keep the enclosure's temperature and humidity levels steady. Jumping spiders prefer temperatures between 70°F and 80°F (21°C and 27°C) and between 50% and 70% of humidity. Consistent monitoring and adjustments guarantee your arachnid friend has a comfortable and stable environment.

Nutrition and Feeding:

As carnivores, jumping spiders need a diet high in small insects. give a varied, suitably sized diet of fruit flies, pinhead crickets, and other small prey that fits their size. It is important to give a balanced nutritional intake to promote the health and well-being of jumping spiders.

Jumping spiders can be picky eaters, so pay special attention to when they eat. For example, they may refuse food during molting or when they are gravid (carrying eggs). You should never overfeed them because this can cause health problems. Fresh water should always be available in a small, shallow dish for drinking.

Positive Interactions and Patience:

Gaining the trust of your jumping spider takes time, patience, and pleasant encounters. You should avoid startling the spider with rapid movements or loud noises, and you should spend some time monitoring its behavior from a distance before attempting direct contact.

Positive interactions begin with placing your hand close to the enclosure without making any abrupt movements. The spider will examine you and get used to your presence. Eventually, you may carefully bring your hand into the enclosure, allowing it to come closer at its own speed.

Consistent, gentle interactions help to build a sense of comfort and trust between you and your jumping spider. If the spider displays signs of concern, such as raising its front legs or backing away, give it room and try again later.

Seeing Behavior and Reacting to It:

To better understand your jumping spider's mood and needs, pay close attention to its behavior. Changes in posture, coloration, and activity level might be signs of a number of different states, including as hunger, stress, or preparation for molting.

Recognize the differences between normal behavior and symptoms of distress. Normal behavior can be characterized by relaxed body posture, bright colors, and active exploration; stress can be characterized by quick movements, defensive postures, or avoidance behaviors.

Creating a Bond via Enhancement:

The mental stimulation and general well-being of your jumping spider can be enhanced by enrichment activities. Occasionally add new things to their environment, like various textures, items to investigate, or small obstacles to climb. These activities allow them to engage in activities that are in line with their natural tendencies.

To provide the jumping spider with a secure and stimulating habitat, you may want to consider creating a supervised exploring area outside the enclosure. Make sure you keep a careful eye on the spider to make sure it is doing well throughout these interactions.

In summary:

Developing a close bond with your jumping spider is an exciting and rewarding experience that calls for commitment, comprehension, and a sincere love for these amazing arachnids. By setting up the right conditions, giving them the care they need, and fostering positive interactions, you can build a solid bond based on mutual respect and trust. Keep an open mind and be patient as you work toward this bond, allowing the relationship to develop naturally over time.

Chapter 7

Common Myths Dispelled About Keeping Jumping Spiders as Pets

With their captivating behaviors and endearing personalities, jumping spiders have become more and more popular as pets in recent years. However, with this increased interest in owning these arachnids as companions, a number of myths and misconceptions have also surfaced, which needs to be debunked in order to guarantee responsible and knowledgeable care for jumping spiders as pets.

Myth 1: Spiders that jump are dangerous

The idea that jumping spiders are dangerous is one of the most common myths about them. In actuality, jumping spiders are usually safe for humans. Their small fangs, which they use to subdue their prey, prevent them from biting humans. When they do bite, the pain is usually no more severe than a mild bee sting. It's also worth noting that allergic reactions to spider bites are very uncommon.

In order to dispel this myth, it is imperative to distinguish between venomous and non-threatening spiders. Jumping spiders are classified as non-threatening, and their presence as pets presents little risk to their owners.

Myth 2: Complicated Enclosures Are Necessary for Leaping Spiders

Another common misconception is that intricate and complex enclosures are necessary to keep jumping spiders as pets. In actuality, these spiders do well in relatively simple setups; all you really need is a small terrarium with adequate ventilation, a suitable substrate, and a few climbing structures. Because jumping spiders are nimble and like to explore, it's more important to provide them with an environment that has vertical elements and hiding spots than it is to have a large horizontal space.

The jumping spider will live in a healthier and less stressful environment if the enclosure is kept simple and easy to maintain. Too many decorations can make it difficult to keep an eye on the behavior and general health of the spider.

Myth 3: Only live prey is necessary for jumping spiders.

While live prey, like fruit flies and small crickets, can provide vital nutrients, providing pre-killed or frozen prey is a practical and safe alternative. The misconception that jumping spiders can only be fed live prey and will not accept pre-killed or frozen alternatives is unfounded. Instead, jumping spiders are opportunistic feeders and can be trained to accept a variety of food sources.

The introduction of a varied diet guarantees nutritional balance and allows for the owner's preferences and convenience. It is important to monitor the feeding response of the spider and modify the diet as necessary. Offering a blend of live and pre-killed prey improves the health of the jumping spider without sacrificing its nutritional requirements.

Myth 4: Pets That Jump Spiders Need Little Upkeep

Although they don't need as much care as larger pets, jumping spiders do have certain needs that need to be met, just like any other living thing. These needs include giving them a balanced diet, keeping an appropriate environment with consistent temperature and humidity levels, and keeping an eye out for any signs of stress or illness in their behavior.

While they may not require daily walks or extensive grooming, jumping spiders do require attentive and responsible care. Regular observation and interaction are key components of responsible ownership. Bonding with a jumping spider involves spending time to understand its habits, preferences, and any changes in behavior that may indicate health issues.

Myth 5: Spiders that Jump Can Live Only on Water

It's a dangerous myth that jumping spiders can only survive on water and don't need to eat live or pre-killed prey. As obligate carnivores, jumping spiders must eat insects to meet their nutritional needs. Although they may drink water droplets, this is not a replacement for their essential diet.

Inadequate nutrition can result in malnourishment, compromised immune systems, and general health deterioration. A healthy diet that is both diverse and balanced and contains appropriate prey is crucial for the welfare of pet jumping spiders.

Myth 6: Spiders that Jump Are Alone and Don't Like to Interact

Jumping spiders are known for being curious and inquisitive, and they frequently show interest in their owners' presence. Despite the common misconception that jumping spiders are solitary and unresponsive to interaction, many owners have reported positive experiences engaging with their arachnid companions.

Even though they might not be as interested in physical affection as more conventional pets, jumping spiders are nonetheless capable of identifying their owners and reacting to stimuli. Good interactions, like putting your hand inside their enclosure very gently or watching them from a distance, can help to build a relationship based on familiarity and trust.

Myth 7: The Lifespan of Jumping Spiders Is Short

The longevity of a jumping spider varies depending on the species; some may live only a few months in captivity, while others can live for over a year. This misconception about jumping spiders' short lifespans is unfounded.

Jumping spiders can have long lives as pets if given the right care, a good home, and a healthy diet. They can also live longer lives if their health is regularly checked and any problems are dealt with early on, which will prolong their companionship.

Myth 8: Spiders That Jump Often Have an Escape Plan

The misconception that jumping spiders are always trying to break out of their enclosures stems from their nimble and acrobatic movements. Although these spiders can jump a great distance, they are not naturally skilled at breaking free.

A well-fitting lid and a secure enclosure are essential for preventing unintentional escapes. You should periodically check the enclosure for any gaps or openings and use secure closures to reduce the possibility of the spider escaping. If you take the right precautions, there is very little chance of a jumping spider escaping.

Myth 9: All Spiders That Jump Are Identical

Another myth is that all jumping spider species are the same, with the same needs and behaviors and different preferences. There are many different species of jumping spiders, some of which are more active than others, and it's important to know the specific requirements and behaviors of the species you have in order to provide the best care possible.

For the purpose of constructing an appropriate and enriching environment, it is imperative to research the unique requirements of your species of jumping spider, including habitat preferences, diet, and environmental conditions.

In summary:

Dispelling common misconceptions about jumping spider behavior, care needs, and potential risks will help both current and prospective owners approach owning these fascinating creatures with more knowledge and empathy. Responsible care builds a positive relationship between humans and their jumping spider companions. The goal of debunking common myths about jumping spiders as pets is to ensure the well-being of these fascinating arachnids.

Chapter 8

The Skill of Perception: Acquiring Knowledge from Your Leaping Spider

The art of observation requires close attention to detail, patience, and an open mind in order to learn from your jumping spider's behaviors, preferences, and innate instincts. Watching a jumping spider can be an enthralling and rewarding experience that not only expands your knowledge of these amazing arachnids but also creates a special bond between you and your tiny companion.

Recognizing the Value of Observation

One of the most important aspects of responsible pet ownership is observation, especially when it comes to jumping spider care. These spry arachnids have complex behaviors and a surprising amount of intelligence, so spending some time observing and analyzing your jumping spider's actions will help you learn a lot about its general temperament, habits, and state of health.

Through active participation and reflection, observation is a dynamic process that goes beyond simple observation. By practicing observation, you may build a stronger bond with your jumping spider, anticipate its needs, and adapt properly to any behavioral changes.

Setting Up the Perfect Setting for Observation:

Assemble a clean, comfortable enclosure with appropriate substrate, climbing structures, and hiding places. A clean and comfortable enclosure encourages the spider to exhibit its natural behaviors, giving you a more accurate understanding of its preferences. This is the first step in effectively observing your jumping spider.

A peaceful, stress-free atmosphere is ideal for true observation, therefore position the enclosure where natural light can reveal the actions of the spider. Steer clear of abrupt loud noises or other disruptions that could shock the spider.

Creating a Schedule:

When it comes to observation, regularity is essential. Create a schedule that includes time set aside for observing and chatting with your jumping spider. Whether it's a few minutes a day or a longer session at particular times, a routine encourages predictability and helps the spider become used to your presence.

Being patient and not rushing these observation sessions is important since jumping spiders can react to changes in their surroundings and startling movements might stress them out. By keeping your routine consistent, you foster a calm environment that supports natural behaviors.

Seeing How People Feed:

Offering a variety of live prey, such as fruit flies or small crickets, and observing the spider's reaction is one of the most fascinating things about jumping spiders. You can learn a lot about their agility and hunting strategies by watching how they approach, capture, and eat prey.

Pay attention to hunting strategies, since jumping spiders have a distinctive way of hunting. They track prey with their keen eyes and make accurate jumps to catch it. The whole stalking to the last pounce display the spider's intellect and flexibility.

Observing Color Shifts and Positions:

Bright and vibrant colors often indicate contentment, while dull or dark colors may suggest stress or discomfort. Jumping spiders are known for their vibrant colors, which can change depending on various factors such as mood, health, and environmental conditions. You should regularly observe your spider's coloration and take note of any changes.

Furthermore, observe the spider's body postures. A relaxed spider will have its legs outstretched, whereas a stressed or defensive spider will draw its legs in and raise its body. Acquiring an understanding of these subtle cues will help you determine the spider's emotional state and react appropriately.

Recognizing Mating Habits:

If you own a pair of jumping spiders, it is imperative that you comprehend their mating habits. Observing the males during their elaborate wooing displays to entice the ladies may be both informative and fascinating.

While female jumping spiders may display receptive behaviors or, in some species, aggressive behavior if they are not interested, males can communicate with potential mates through complex leg movements, visual displays, and even vibrations. Paying close attention to these interactions allows you to appreciate the complexity of their reproductive rituals and communication.

Keeping an eye on Web-building Activities:

Even though they do not weave webs like some other arachnids, jumping spiders can make silk for a variety of uses, such building egg sacs or shelters. Seeing these silk-related behaviors reveals something about their versatility and inventiveness.

You may observe how versatile silk is in the life of a jumping spider by closely observing some of its many uses, such as creating retreats or sleeping quarters where the spiders can take sanctuary, anchoring themselves when hunting, or securing prey.

Keep Track of Molting Cycles:

Like other arachnids, jumping spiders must molt in order to grow and shed their exoskeleton; this is a delicate time for the spider and should be carefully observed; it may become lethargic, lose interest in food, and seek out a safe place during this time.

Creating a calm, disturbance-free environment for your spider to molt is crucial. You should also watch how it moves in the lead-up to the molt, during the molt, and in the aftermath. Keeping track of the frequency and circumstances of molting will help you learn more about your spider's growth and development.

Respectful Interaction:

Positive interaction is just as important to learning from your jumping spider as observation, which usually entails observing from a distance. Slowly place your hand within the enclosure and let the spider come to you at its own speed. See how it reacts to your motions and presence.

A gentle and respectful approach to handling your jumping spider will help you both develop a stronger bond. Avoid abrupt gestures or attempts to handle the spider aggressively, since jumping spiders may interpret these acts as threats and become stressed or protective.

Recording Actions:

Keep a thorough log or journal to better understand the behaviors of your jumping spider. Record observations, color changes, feeding reactions, and any noteworthy events. This documentation becomes a useful reference over time, enabling you to monitor trends, spot possible health problems, and record developmental milestones.

Provide information about the enclosure's modifications, prey kinds, and environmental circumstances. By documenting information in a methodical manner, you will be better equipped to make judgments about your spider's care and welfare.

Acquiring Knowledge from Unique Characters

Even though they are members of the same family, jumping spiders can have distinct personalities and tastes. Some may be more gregarious and inquisitive than others, and observing them requires being able to identify and value these individual variances.

You can identify your jumping spider's unique personality traits by devoting time to studying and interacting with it. Certain spiders may be more sociable with people, while others would rather be observed from a distance. By learning these subtleties, you can adjust your care and attention to your spider's specific needs.

Teaching People by Observation:

When you share your observations with others through social media, online forums, or educational platforms, you add to the body of knowledge about these amazing species, which goes beyond the benefits of personal enrichment.

Posting images, videos, or stories about your observations can encourage curiosity and admiration for these small, fascinating friends. By busting misconceptions and providing factual information on jumping spiders, you can contribute to the development of a favorable attitude toward arachnids as pets.

In summary:

Developing the skill of observation is a dynamic and fulfilling hobby that makes owning a jumping spider a rich and educational experience. By making the time to observe and learn from your arachnid companion, you will gain a deeper understanding of its needs and behaviors as well as a meaningful and unique bond.

By watching, you learn about all the subtle aspects of your jumping spider's world, from its vivid color changes to its nimble hunting strategies. With this increased awareness, you can better attend to its needs, create a happy environment, and support its general well-being.

Accept the chance to learn from the little but fascinating world of your jumping spider by approaching observation with patience, respect, and an open mind. Allow the art of observation to lead you on a voyage of exploration and connection with one of nature's most fascinating arachnids.

Chapter 9

Selecting the Correct Jumping Spider Species for Yourself

The choice of which species of jumping spider to keep as a pet is an exciting one that requires careful consideration of many factors, such as size, behavior, and habitat preferences. Jumping spiders are members of the Salticidae family, which is diverse and contains many species, each with unique characteristics. In order to make an informed decision, it is important to research your options, comprehend the requirements of various species, and match your preferences and level of experience as a spider keeper.

Investigating Species of Jumping Spiders:

Research your options thoroughly before selecting a species of jumping spider. Although the family Salticidae contains many species, not all of them are good for captivity. Some species of jumping spiders that are kept in captivity are Phidippus regius, also known as the regal jumping spider, Marpissa muscosa, also known as the peacock jumping spider, and Phidippus audax, the bold jumping spider.

Take into account attributes like size, color, behavior, and preferred environment; certain jumping spider species may be more gregarious and inquisitive than others. Keep in mind the particular maintenance demands of each species, such as humidity levels, temperature, and food requirements.

Dimensions and Look:
The size and appearance of jumping spiders vary greatly; some species are quite little, with a body length of about 0.1 inches, while others can grow to be as large as 0.75

inches or larger. Depending on the size of the spider, handling and enclosure requirements will vary.

Jumping spider species also differ greatly in terms of coloration; some are recognized for their vivid and eye-catching hues, while others have more muted or mysterious designs. Think about your personal taste in design and whether you want a spider that stands out or one that disappears into its surroundings.

Conduct and Degree of Activity:

Jumping spiders are known for their lively and curious habits, while different species may show different degrees of activity and interest. Certain species may be more likely to explore their enclosures and engage with their owners, while other species may be more reticent.

A species like the bold jumping spider (Phidippus audax) or the regal jumping spider (Phidippus regius) might be a good choice if you're looking for a high-activity, bold-natured jumping spider. If you're more of a laid-back, perceptive kind of person, you could look into species with a calmer temperament.

Preferences for Habitat:

For the purpose of creating a suitable and enriching environment, it is important to understand the natural habitat of the species of jumping spider you are interested in. While some jumping spiders prefer grassy areas, others live in forested areas or on leaf litter, imitating their natural habitat in captivity helps create a more comfortable and stimulating living space.

Because many jumping spiders are arboreal and like to climb, take into account the enclosure's verticality.

Provide suitable climbing and hiding structures, such branches, twigs, or leaves. Choose substrates that complement the natural habitat of the spider, like coconut fiber or peat moss.

Requirements for temperature and humidity:

Different species of jumping spiders prefer different temperatures and humidity levels; find out what the ideal conditions are by researching the native range of the species you are interested in. Generally speaking, most jumping spiders do best in temperatures between 70°F and 80°F (21°C and 27°C) and between 50% and 70% of humidity.

Keeping the enclosure's temperature and humidity levels consistent with a trustworthy thermometer and hygrometer is important for the health of the spider as a whole, as well as its activity level, eating habits, and success rate during molting.

Choosing Your Meals:

Research the feeding habits of the species you are interested in to ensure you can provide a suitable and varied diet. Jumping spiders are carnivorous and feed on a variety of small insects. While many species readily accept common prey items such as fruit flies and pinhead crickets, some may have specific dietary preferences.

Think about what kinds of prey are readily available where you live, as well as whether you feel comfortable providing a variety of foods for your jumping spider. You should also pay attention to the way the spider eats because some species of jumping spiders have distinct ways of hunting, like ambushing or actively pursuing their prey.

Managing Points to Remember:

Because of their small size and delicate nature, handling jumping spiders needs to be done carefully and gently. Although some species can handle handling to a certain extent, it is important to put the safety of the spider first. Think about whether you feel comfortable handling a species that might be more likely to investigate your hand or one that would rather stay in its enclosure.

Remember that handling jumping spiders entails the risk of accidental escape or injury due to their fast and agile nature. If handling is necessary, select a species that is known for its calm temperament and approach them patiently and carefully. Steer clear of sudden movements and create a safe and controlled environment for interactions.

Experience Level:

When selecting a species of jumping spider to keep, take into account your level of experience level as a spider keeper. Certain species may be more tolerant of small care errors, while others may have particular needs requiring more experience. If you are a novice, it is best to start with a species that is well-known for being resilient and adaptable to captive environments.

Regardless of skill level, careful research and a dedication to responsible care are vital for the well-being of your jumping spider. Expert spider keepers may be drawn to more difficult or uncommon species that require specialized care.

Accessibility and Lawfulness:

Verify the availability and legality of the jumping spider species you wish to keep. Certain species might be easier to come by in the pet trade, while others might be more difficult to find or need special permits. Make sure you are obtaining your spider in an ethical and legal manner, and think about supporting reliable breeders or suppliers.

Look into any laws or ordinances pertaining to the possession of jumping spiders as pets in your area. Some species may be protected, and obtaining them without the necessary permits may result in legal ramifications. When purchasing a jumping spider, put the welfare of the animal first and follow ethical guidelines.

Online and Community Resources:

Join the community of jumpers and make use of online resources to learn from and get advice from seasoned keepers. Social media groups, forums, and specialized websites offer excellent venues for talking about certain species, exchanging observations, and answering questions.

Seek advice and guidance from knowledgeable jump spider aficionados. Gaining knowledge from others' experiences can provide important insights into the upkeep and habits of various species, enabling you to make an educated choice.

Frequently Housed Leaping Spider Species:

Bold Jumping Spider (Phidippus audax): Distinguished by its eye-catching black and white markings, this bold jumping spider is a favorite among enthusiasts. Its bold and inquisitive nature often results in interaction behaviors, making it a good option for anybody seeking an engaging and energetic companion.

The regal-looking Phidippus regius is a species of jumping spider that has bright colors, such as metallic blues and greens, and a tranquil demeanor, which makes it a wonderful choice for people who like their spiders to be more watchful and laid back.

Peacock jumping spiders, or Marpissa muscosa, are a visually striking species that are distinguished by their intricate and colorful abdominal patterns. Although they may be a bit more reserved than some other jumping spiders, their striking appearance makes them a sought-after choice.

Hentzia palmarum, also known as the Zebra Jumping Spider, is a species of jumping spider that is smaller in size and has a distinctive appearance. It is named for its characteristic black and white striped patterns and is commonly found in grassy areas. It is also known for its agility. The Apache jumping spider, or Phidippus apacheanus, is a native of North America. Its coloring is a mixture of brown and white. This species might be a good fit for people looking for a jumping spider that is more vibrant and engaged because of its active and curious character.

In summary:

Consideration should be given to a number of variables when selecting the appropriate species of jumping spider for you, such as size, behavior, preferred environment, and experience level. Providing the best care and building a healthy relationship with your jumping spider require extensive research and knowledge of the unique requirements of each species.

Each species adds something special and charming to the world of spider keeping, whether you are drawn to the brave and gregarious activities of the bold jumping spider, the majestic appearance of the Phidippus regius, or the eye-catching patterns of the peacock jumping spider. Your experience of caring for and learning from these fascinating arachnids can be beneficial if your tastes match those of the selected species.

Chapter 10

Fascinating Information about Leaping Spiders That Will Astound You

Among the most fascinating and captivating arachnids are jumping spiders, which belong to the Salticidae family. These small spiders astonish both enthusiasts and researchers with their sharp vision, dexterous motions, and fascinating habits. Investigating the world of jumping spiders exposes a plethora of fascinating details that illuminate their exceptional adaptations, creative hunting techniques, and intricate social activities.

1. Masters of Vision:

Unlike many other spider species, jumping spiders are recognized for their remarkable vision. These spiders can precisely discern distance and depth because to their stereoscopic vision, which is made possible by their huge, forward-facing eyes. Especially well-developed and functioning comparable to human eyes are the major eyes, also called anterior median eyes.

Their keen vision is important for communication, navigation, and mate detection in addition to being essential for hunting. Jumping spiders' optical range is wider than that of humans; they can even see ultraviolet light. Their accomplishment as quick-witted and proficient hunters is a result of their extraordinary vision.

2. Silk Absent Webs:

Though many spiders are renowned for their capacity to spin webs, jumping spiders are an anomaly. Rather than creating intricate webs to capture their food, jumping spiders actively seek out and attack their prey. They still make silk, though, for a variety of uses.

Silk is used by jumping spiders to produce protective egg sacs, draglines for protection, and shelters. Unlike web-building spiders, leaping spiders create silk that has numerous functional roles in their life. It is not as sticky.

3. The Technique of Leaping:

As their name suggests, leaping spiders may jump very far. They can leap astonishingly far because to their strong rear legs, especially while they're hunting. Certain creatures can jump 50 times their body length and traverse great distances. Their exceptional physical prowess allows them to precisely locate prey and navigate their environment.

Jumping spiders use silk to anchor themselves before taking a leap, forming a safe haven. As a safety precaution, this silk safety rope makes sure that even in the unlikely event that they miss their aim, they can easily return to where they started without running the risk of falling.

4. Astute Hunters:

Among the smartest arachnids are thought to be jumping spiders. Their sophisticated actions, problem-solving techniques, and hunting tactics all demonstrate their high level of cognitive ability. Jumping spiders are patient and well-prepared predators that frequently approach their prey deliberately before making a dramatic leap.

Experiments carried out by researchers have shown that jumping spiders are capable of learning. In these trials, spiders are trained to detect particular visual stimuli or to navigate mazes. In the world of arachnids, the spiders' constant adaptation and memory retention demonstrate their intelligence.

5. Customs of Courtship:

Jumping spiders perform complex displays and communication between possible mates as part of their complicated courtship rituals. In order to draw in females, male jumping spiders frequently put on visual displays and employ particular body gestures. Vibrant color changes, leg waving, and even rhythmic vibrations sent through the substrate can all be a part of these displays.

In response, women could act receptively, showing that they are interested in the potential partner. Jumping spider courtship rituals differ from species to species and can be aesthetically pleasing as well as scientifically significant. Researching these customs reveals details on the Salticidae family's reproductive and communication tactics.

6. Bright Color Scheme:

In addition to being smart and nimble, jumping spiders have an amazing spectrum of colors. Numerous species have eye-catching coloration that varies from strong patterns of black, white, and red to metallic greens and blues. These hues are used for communication, mate attraction, and camouflage, among other things.

In several species, males use bright colors to attract females during courtship. Some jumping spiders can also alter their coloring in response to external stimuli or emotion. Not only are these color shifts physically striking, but they also play a part in their complex social behaviors.

7. Masters of Mimicry:

Because they can change their color and behavior, jumping spiders are effective mimics of other animals. Since ants tend to be less attractive to potential predators, some jumping spiders imitate them in order to evade being eaten. Jumping spiders may traverse through ant colonies without drawing attention to themselves by mimicking the movements and behaviors of ants.

Their methods of hunting are also mimicry. Certain jumping spiders imitate their prey's appearance and movements in order to sneak up on their victim. This cunning action demonstrates jumping spiders' adaptability and versatility in the intricate environments they live in.

8. intricate social structures

Despite their reputation for being solitary, certain species of jumping spider display intricate social behaviors. There have been cases where jumping spider colonies have been seen coexisting in public areas. These colonies could have several generations of individuals participating in cooperative behaviors including sharing prey and guarding the common area.

Different species of jumping spiders have different colony dynamics, and not all of them display social behaviors. The presence of social structures, however, casts doubt on conventional theories of spider behavior and emphasizes how complex and varied jumping spider communities are.

9. Communication through Audition:

Although their major means of communication is vision, some species of jumping spiders may also employ aural cues, according to recent research. Researchers have found that some jumping spiders vibrate when they land on leaves or other surfaces, sending out audio signals that could be used as a kind of communication.

These vibrations can be involved in mating rituals, territorial conflicts, or courtship. The finding of auditory communication highlights jumping spiders' versatility in a variety of ecological contexts by adding even another level to their extremely complicated repertoire of activities.

10. Specialized Mating Techniques:

Numerous mating techniques are used by jumping spiders, which helps to increase the success of their reproduction. Some species display unusual actions in addition to the complex courtship rituals already discussed in order to improve their chances of successful mating. As part of their courtship display, certain male jumping spiders, for instance, give females gifts wrapped in silk, such as silk decorations or prey.

Male jumping spiders occasionally use "sneaky" mating strategies. Some approach and mate with unsuspecting males by imitating the look of females. The jumping spider family's sophisticated and diverse reproductive adaptations are exemplified by these cunning tactics.

11. Differential Ecological Niche:

Vibrant forests, grassy meadows, urban settings, and other natural niches have all been successfully invaded by jumping spiders. Their widespread distribution is facilitated by their capacity to adapt to many habitats. While some species live in vegetation or on rocky surfaces, others prefer the litter of leaves.

Jumping spiders are important to the ecosystem because they can live in a variety of settings and are both predators and prey. Understanding their distribution and ecological roles helps one better understand the complex web of relationships that exist within ecosystems.

12. Taking Care of Parents:

Known for their remarkable maternal care, jumping spiders exhibit a behavior not often associated with spiders. A female jumping spider creates a silk sac to enclose her eggs when she lays them. To protect the eggs from prospective predators, the female guards the sac and may move it with her.

Spiderlings hatch and come out of the sac under the mother's continued protection and direction. This unusual display of mother care by jumping spiders emphasizes the commitment these creatures make to the survival of their young.

13. Variety in Diet:

As carnivores, jumping spiders consume a variety of small arthropods in their diet. They hunt with precision, frequently ambushing, stalking, and jumping on their target. Ants, other spiders, flies, and mosquitoes are examples of common prey.

Jumping spiders play an important ecological role as natural pest controls because of their varied food. By feeding on a range of insects, they support the management of potentially dangerous pest populations and aid in the preservation of ecological equilibrium.

14. Limited Lifespan:

In comparison to certain other arachnids, jumping spiders usually have shorter lifespans despite their amazing actions and adaptations. Jumping spiders can live anywhere from a few months to a little over a year, depending on the species. A spider's lifespan is influenced by various factors, including food, molting success, and environmental conditions.

Jumping spiders have comparatively short lifespans, which emphasizes the value of effective reproduction techniques and the contribution of each generation to the species' survival.

15. Diversity Around the World:

Jumping spiders are remarkably diverse, with over 6,000 species identified and spread all over the world. Because of their ability to adapt to different surroundings and their distinct habits, a wide variety of species have evolved. Jumping spiders have spread to practically every continent, inhabiting a variety of environments from dry deserts to tropical rainforests.

Scientists have a wealth of research opportunities to better understand the evolutionary processes that have produced the jumping spider family due to the diversity of these spiders across the globe. Specific characteristics and adaptations have evolved in each species in response to its own ecological niche.

In summary:

Jumping spiders never cease to astound scientists and enthusiasts with their remarkable vision, intellect, and intriguing habits. These arachnids demonstrate the intricacy and adaptability of the natural world through their varied ecological functions, elaborate courting rituals, and sophisticated hunting skills.

By exploring the fascinating details regarding jumping spiders, we may better understand the distinctive characteristics that make them one of the most fascinating and varied families of spiders. Jumping spiders provide a window into the complex web of life, where these small arachnids play important roles in preserving ecological balance and adding to the planet's rich variety. This is demonstrated by their remarkable visual abilities as well as their parental care activities."

FAQs

1. Is it wise to keep jumping spiders as pets?

A: Because of their small size, interesting habits, and low maintenance needs, jumping spiders do really make wonderful pets.

2. What is the diet of jumping spiders?

A: The main food source for jumping spiders is small arthropods, such as flies and mosquitoes.

3. Can humans be bitten by jumping spiders?

A: Although jumping spiders can bite when prompted, humans are only mildly irritated by their poison.

4. How large can a jumping spider grow?

A: Generally speaking, jumping spiders are tiny, measuring anything from a few millimeters to about two centimeters.

5. Do jumping spiders have poison?

A: Although jumping spiders are poisonous, their venom is meant to immobilize victims rather than kill people.

6. Q: What makes the eyesight of jumping spiders special?

A: Jumping spiders sense a broad spectrum of colors, including ultraviolet light, thanks to their remarkable vision.

7. Do jumping spiders know who owns them?

A: Although there is disagreement, some research indicates that jumping spiders may be able to identify and learn about certain humans.

8. What is the lifespan of a jumping spider?

A: Although jumping spider lifespans vary by species, they usually last anywhere from several months to more than a year.

9. Do jumping spiders pose a threat to people?

A: Jumping spiders are renowned for their inquisitive and non-threatening demeanor, and they are typically not aggressive.

10. What kind of silk do jumping spiders make?

A: It is true that jumping spiders make silk, which they use to make draglines, shelters, and occasionally egg sacs.

11. Question: Are jumping spiders able to jump very far?
- A: Contrary to what their name suggests, jumping spiders only make brief, safe leaps; they employ silk threads as safety lines.

12. What kind of environment is ideal for jumping spiders?
- A: Jumping spiders live in grassy meadows, gardens, residences, and woodlands, among other places.

13. How do jumping spiders exchange messages?
- A: Chemical signals, vibrations, and visual displays are the three ways that jumping spiders communicate.

14. Do jumping spiders undergo molting?

A: In order to expand, jumping spiders do indeed molt, revealing a larger exoskeleton underneath.

15. Can groups of jumping spiders be maintained together?
- A: Because jumping spiders have a tendency to become cannibalistic and territorial, it is typically not advised to keep them in groups.

16. Q: How do jumping spiders court one another?
- A: To entice females, male jumping spiders engage in complex courtship displays that include visual cues and rhythmic motions.

17. A: How do jumping spiders go on hunts?
- A: Using their keen vision to find and ambush insects, jumping spiders hunt by stalking and jumping on their prey.

18. Q: Do leaping spiders belong to separate species?

A: It is true that there are thousands of species of jumping spiders known to science, each with distinct traits.

19. Q: Is it possible to train leaping spiders?

A few research indicate that jumping spiders have a limited capacity for learning from their experiences.

20. Q: Like other spiders, do jumping spiders spin webs?

A: Although they don't construct elaborate webs to capture food, jumping spiders do utilize silk for a variety of purposes, including building shelters.

Can jumping spiders survive indoors? 21.

A comfortable atmosphere and access to sufficient prey are necessary for jumping spiders to survive indoors.

22. Q: Do jumping spiders spend the night?

- A: Diurnal in nature, jumping spiders are active during the day and sleep at night.

23. What kind of food is best for a pet jumping spider?
- A: Provide small live insects, like fruit flies, pinhead crickets, or tiny ants, as food for your pet jumping spider.

24. What is the range at which jumping spiders can detect their prey?
A: It's true that jumping spiders have exceptional eyesight and can spot possible prey from a distance.

25. Is there a predatory species of jumping spider?
- A: Larger spiders, birds, and certain insects are predators of jumping spiders.

26. Q: Are jumping spiders able to climb glass?

A: Yes, thanks to their unique leg structures, jumping spiders can crawl on glass surfaces.

Q: Do jumping spiders go into hibernation?
- A: Although they do not hibernate, jumping spiders may become less active in colder climates.

28. Q: How frequently should the enclosure for my jumping spider be cleaned?
- A: Depending on the enclosure's size and the spider's requirements, clean the enclosure on a regular basis to get rid of trash, molted exoskeletons, and uneaten prey.

29. Is it possible for jumping spiders to coexist with other types of spiders?
- A: Because jumping spiders can become territorial, it is not advisable to keep them in the same home as other spider species.

30. Q: How long does a captive jumping spider live?

A: Given the right care, a jumping spider's lifespan in captivity can surpass a year.

31. Q: Do jumping spiders have color perception?

- A: A wide range of hues, including ultraviolet light, may be seen by jumping spiders.

32. Q: Can jumping spiders contract any diseases?

A: Although jumping spiders are comparatively disease-resistant, stress and bad husbandry practices can compromise their health.

33. What self-defense mechanisms do jumping spiders employ?

- A: Jumping spiders can use their dexterity to avoid danger, and some species can fool predators by appearing like ants.

34. Q: Do backward-jumping spiders exist?

- A: Spiders that jump have the ability to change the direction of their jumps, so they can leap backward if necessary.

35. Can I take care of my jumping spider pet?

A: Although most jumping spiders are not aggressive, it is nevertheless advisable to handle them carefully to prevent stress and possible harm.

36. What kind of self-grooming do jumping spiders do?

- A: To groom themselves and get dirt and debris off their bodies, jumping spiders utilize unique legs and mouthparts.

37. What kind of surface is appropriate for an enclosure housing jumping spiders?

- A: For a comfortable and humidity-retaining surface, choose a substrate such as peat moss or coconut coir for a jumping spider habitat.

38. Q: Are jumping spiders able to distinguish between different human voices?
A: There isn't much data to support the theory that jumping spiders can differentiate between various human speech patterns.

39. What kind of personalities do jumping spiders have?
A: Individual behavioral variations do occur, but whether or not jumping spiders have unique personalities is up for debate.

40. What is the process by which jumping spiders adjust to environmental changes?

A: Although jumping spiders are able to adapt to changes in their surroundings, abrupt or drastic alterations are to be avoided.

41. Question: How can I give my pet jumping spider water?
- A: To provide your jumping spider with access to water, mist an area of the enclosure or provide a tiny water dish with a moist sponge.

42. Q: Do jumping spiders have night vision?
- A: Although jumping spiders' vision is well suited for low light, they are not evolved to see in total darkness.

43. Q: Do jumping spiders require any particular temperature?
Maintain an enclosure temperature of between 70 and 80°F (21-27°C) for the majority of species of jumping spiders.

44. What is the mode of communication used by jumping spiders?

- A: During courting, jumping spiders convey messages visually through displays and body language.

45. Q: Are jumping spiders able to identify patterns or images?

- A: Research indicates that jumping spiders might be able to identify patterns or images, which would help them learn.

46. Is it possible for jumping spiders to survive without exposure to sunlight?

- A: Although jumping spiders don't need direct sunlight to survive, they do need a well-lit space.

47. Q: If jumping spiders are siblings, may they be kept together?

- A: House jumping spiders separately to avoid possible confrontations, even if siblings may tolerate one another for a while.

48. Is there a certain type of prey that jumping spiders prefer?

- A: Jumping spiders can adapt to a variety of food items depending on availability, although they typically prefer small, soft-bodied insects.

49. Q: Are leaping spiders able to detect their own reflections and react accordingly?

A: Certain jumping spiders may exhibit territorial behavior or courtship movements in response to their reflection.

50. What indicate that a jumping spider is in good health?

- A: A well-groomed jumping spider is consistently hungry for prey, behaves in an active manner, and displays these traits.